TOADS

Julie Murray

Big Buddy Books

An Imprint of Abdo Publishing
abdobooks.com

abdobooks.com

Published by Abdo Publishing, a division of ABDO, PO Box 398166, Minneapolis, Minnesota 55439.
Copyright © 2020 by Abdo Consulting Group, Inc. International copyrights reserved in all countries.
No part of this book may be reproduced in any form without written permission from the publisher.
Big Buddy Books™ is a trademark and logo of Abdo Publishing.

Printed in the United States of America, North Mankato, Minnesota
052019
092019

 THIS BOOK CONTAINS
RECYCLED MATERIALS

Design: Sarah DeYoung, Mighty Media, Inc.
Production: Mighty Media, Inc.
Editor: Liz Salzmann
Cover Photograph: Shutterstock
Interior Photographs: iStockphoto (p. 27); Shutterstock (pp. 4–5, 6, 8, 9, 10, 11, 13, 14, 15, 17, 18–19,
    20, 23, 25, 28)

Library of Congress Control Number: 2018939895

Publisher's Cataloging-in-Publication Data
Names: Murray, Julie, author.
Title: Toads / by Julie Murray.
Description: Minneapolis, Minnesota : Abdo Publishing, 2020. I Series:
    Animal kingdom I Includes online resources and index.
Identifiers: ISBN 9781532116551 (lib.bdg.) I ISBN 9781532158049 (ebook)
Subjects: LCSH: Toads--Juvenile literature. I Toads--Behavior--Juvenile
    literature. I Amphibians--Juvenile literature.
Classification: DDC 597.87--dc23

Contents

TOADS ARE AMPHIBIANS

Toads are **amphibians**. Amphibians have **spines**. They have bare skin with no feathers or hair. Baby amphibians live in water. Adult amphibians live on land. Frogs and salamanders are amphibians too.

Toads live in water
and on land.

Toads can live everywhere except areas that are cold most of the time.

Toads live in many places around the world. They can live in forests, meadows, and backyards.

TOAD OR FROG?

People often **confuse** toads with frogs. But these **amphibians** are different in many ways.

Toads walk and make short hops.

Most toads cannot hop as far as frogs. Most toads have round bodies and short legs. Most frogs are **slender** with longer legs.

Frogs can leap long distances.

Toads have thick, bumpy skin. Frogs have smooth skin. Toads can live away from water. Frogs stay near water.

Toads have bumpy skin.

Frogs have smooth skin.

11

WHAT TOADS LOOK LIKE

There are many different kinds of toads. Most toads are between two and four inches (5 and 10 cm) long. But the **marine** toad can be nine inches (23 cm) long.

The marine toad is also called the cane toad.

13

Many toads are brown and green.
But the fire-bellied toad has a
red-orange belly.

A fire-bellied toad

Toads and Warts

Toads have bumps on their skin.
Sometimes, people call these bumps
warts. But these bumps are not really
warts. And people cannot
get warts from
touching
toads.

EATING

Toads eat **insects**, spiders, and worms. Toads catch food with their sticky tongues. After catching food, toads swallow it whole. Toads can eat a lot in only a few minutes.

It takes less than half a second for a toad to catch food with its tongue.

17

AMERICAN TOADS

American toads are mostly brown. They may be gray or a dull red too. They often have stripes on their backs.

A special throat pouch helps the American toad croak loudly.

Some American toads make burrows in rotting logs.

American toads live in the United States and Canada. They live in woody areas and backyards. During the winter, American toads **hibernate** in **burrows**.

EASTERN SPADEFOOT TOADS

Eastern spadefoot toads are brown with two stripes on their backs. These toads are named after the "spades" on their back feet. These "spades" help them dig into the ground.

Eastern spadefoot toads dig burrows in mud and sand.

Eastern spadefoot toads live in the United States. They live in sandy places. These toads stay in their **burrows** during the day. They often come out at night and after it rains.

Bad-Tasting Toads

Toads have bad-tasting skin. A toad's bad taste helps to keep it safe from enemies. Some snakes and birds do not want to eat bad-tasting toads.

STAGES OF LIFE

Female toads can lay between 100 and 20,000 eggs at one time. Most toads lay their eggs in water. Midwife toads are different. The male midwife toad carries his **mate's** eggs. He brings the eggs to water before they **hatch**.

Male midwife toads carry eggs on their backs.

Tadpoles are also called polliwogs.

Tadpoles hatch from toad eggs. They look like small fish. Tadpoles live in water and eat tiny water plants.

Over time, a tadpole changes into a toad. It grows legs and **lungs**. And a tadpole loses its tail. After these changes, the young toad can live on land.

Glossary

amphibian (am-FIH-bee-uhn)—an animal that lives part of its life in water and part of its life on land.

burrow—an animal's underground home.

confuse—to mistake one thing for something else.

hatch—to be born from an egg.

hibernate—to sleep or rest during the winter months.

insect—a small animal that has six legs and three main parts to its body.

lungs—body parts that help the body breathe.

marine—having to do with the sea.

mate—a partner to join with in order to reproduce, or have babies.

slender—thin or narrow.

spine—backbone.

tadpole—a baby toad.

wart—a lump on the skin.

Online Resources

Booklinks
NONFICTION NETWORK
FREE! ONLINE NONFICTION RESOURCES

To learn more about toads, please visit **abdobooklinks.com** or scan this QR code. These links are routinely monitored and updated to provide the most current information available.

Index